Scholastic Success With Maps

Contents

BY LINDA WARD BEECH

SCHOLASTIC
PROFESSIONAL BOOKS

Using a Map

A map is a picture of part or all of Earth. Because maps provide all kinds of information, they are useful tools in helping you learn about the world.

Like this photo taken from an airplane, maps are pictures of Earth as seen from above.

People have been making maps for thousands of years. The first maps were simply scratches in the dirt or sand. The oldest maps still in existence were drawn on wet clay that was then baked in the sun. Today, maps are much more complex. Mapmakers use aerial photographs and satellite images to make accurate pictures of Earth.

A map shows a large area in a small space. So mapmakers use symbols to represent buildings, highways, cities, and many other things. Be sure to check the map legend to find out what each symbol stands for. A map legend is also called a map key.

An important symbol on a map is the **compass rose**. The compass rose shows the four cardinal directions—north, south, east, and west—and the four intermediate directions—northeast, southeast, southwest, and northwest. Many maps have a **scale** to help you figure out how far it is between places. Use the map scale to measure distances on a map in miles or kilometers.

The Babylonians made this clay map of the world about 2,500 years ago. The Babylonians lived in Mesopotamia, where Iraq is today.

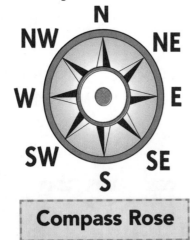

Compass Rose

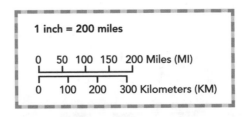

1 inch = 200 miles

0   50 100 150   200 Miles (MI)

0   100   200   300 Kilometers (KM)

Scale of Miles

Downtown Milwaukee

Key

- 🚶 River walk
- 🛣️ **43** Interstate highway
- 🛣️ **41** State highway
- ■ Place of interest
- ■ Park

19th St.

6th St.

Pabst Mansion

Wells St.

Wisconsin Ave.

Greater Milwaukee Convention and Visitors Bureau

Public Museum

Grand Avenue Mall

Marcus Center for the Performing Arts

Water St.

Milwaukee River

Michigan St.

Milwaukee St.

Betty Brinn Children's Museum

Milwaukee Art Museum

Lincoln Memorial Dr.

Lake Michigan

←To Miller Park and Wisconsin State Fair Park

Menomonee River

94 41

94 43 41 18 794 794

NW N NE
W E
SW S SE

Scale: 0 — 1/2 Mile

MAP READER'S TIP

The word "map" comes from the Latin word *mappa*, which means napkin or cloth. During the Middle Ages, when Latin was spoken, most maps were made of cloth.

Use the map to answer these questions.

1. What does this symbol 🚶 mean? _____
   Along what body of water is this on the map? _____

2. Near what lake is the art museum? _____
   Is it on the east or west side of the city? _____

3. What building is at the intersection of 19th Street and Wisconsin Avenue?_____

4. About how far is it from this building to the Visitors Bureau? _____

5. What interstate highway would you take to visit Miller Park?_____

6. In which direction from Lake Michigan is the Wisconsin State Fair Park?_____

7. Where might you go to see a concert? _____

8. Milwaukee has a good harbor and is an important Great Lakes port.
   How do you think its location helped the city grow?_____

   _____

Globes and Hemispheres

The best model of Earth is a globe. That's because both a globe and Earth are shaped like a sphere. A globe shows that Earth's surface is covered mostly with water. Earth has four large bodies of water called oceans.

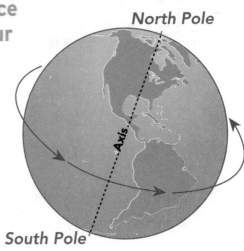

A globe shows how Earth rotates, or turns, on an imaginary center line called an **axis**. At the ends of this line are the North and South poles. The direction of north is toward the North Pole, and the direction of south is toward the South Pole.

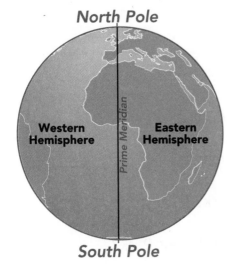

Look closely at a globe and you'll see lines running between the North Pole and the South Pole. These are called lines of longitude or meridians. The Prime Meridian divides Earth into two halves called **hemispheres**. On one side of the **Prime Meridian** is the Eastern Hemisphere and on the other side is the Western Hemisphere.

The lines that run east and west on a globe are called lines of latitude. These lines run parallel to the **equator**. The equator is a line of latitude that runs around the center of Earth and divides it into the Northern and Southern hemispheres.

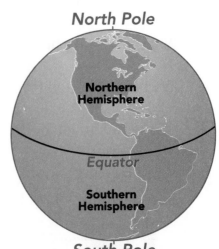

Here are four views of a globe showing the four hemispheres.

Northern Hemisphere

Southern Hemisphere

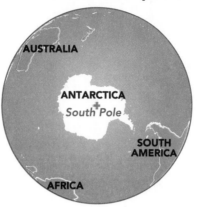

Western Hemisphere

Eastern Hemisphere

MAP READER'S TIP

Some historians think the first globe was made in 1492, the same year that Christopher Columbus reached the Americas. However, this globe, made by the cartographer Martin Behaim, did not show the Americas.

1. In which hemisphere is the North Pole? _____

2. What is the name of the line that is equally distant from the North and South Poles? _____

3. What direction is toward the South Pole? _____

4. In which hemispheres is Australia? _____

5. Name a continent in both the Southern and Western hemispheres. _____

6. What is the Prime Meridian? _____

7. In which directions do lines of latitude run? _____

Projections of the World

Here's a challenge for you. Take an orange and try to peel its skin off in one large piece. Then try to place the orange skin on a sheet of paper so that it lies flat without any spaces.

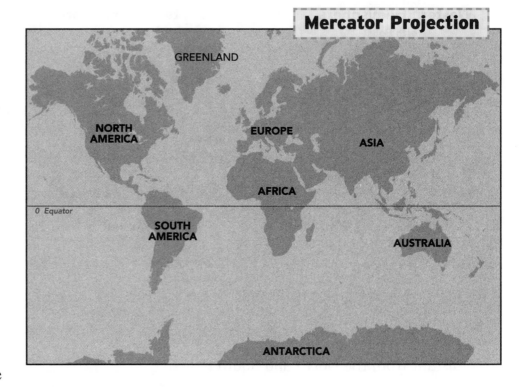

Mercator Projection

GREENLAND

NORTH AMERICA

EUROPE

ASIA

AFRICA

0 Equator

SOUTH AMERICA

AUSTRALIA

ANTARCTICA

This is the same kind of challenge that mapmakers face when they try to draw a picture of Earth on a flat sheet of paper. The shapes and sizes of land and water areas become distorted. It is also hard to represent distances between places accurately. So mapmakers have created different ways of drawing Earth on paper. These views are called **projections**.

You can see three map projections on these pages. One of the most common is a **Mercator projection**. It was developed in 1569 by a German geographer named Gerardus Mercator. His map shows the true shapes of Earth's land, but it distorts sizes—especially near the poles. On a Mercator projection, Greenland looks as large as South America. In fact, South America is eight times larger than Greenland!

Another projection looks a little like the peel of an orange. This is called an **interrupted projection**. While the size and shape of land and water areas are fairly accurate, the oceans and Antarctica are split up.

On a **polar projection**, the North or South Pole is at the center of the map. These maps are accurate in the center, but shapes and distances are distorted at the edges.

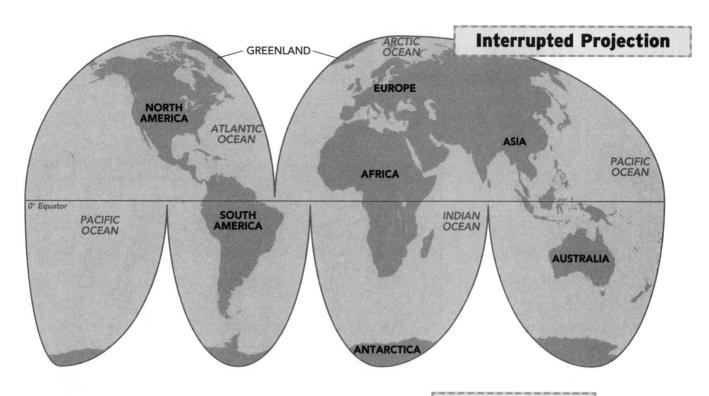

Interrupted Projection

1. What is the shape of the polar projection? _____

2. Is North America more accurate on the Mercator or polar projection?

   _____

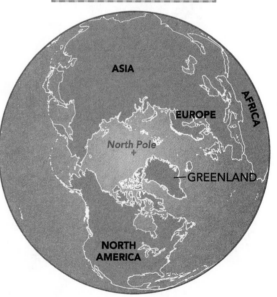

Polar Projection

3. What hemisphere does the polar projection show?_____
   What other hemisphere could a polar projection show?_____

4. On which map is Greenland most accurate? _____

5. Why is it difficult to see Antarctica on the interrupted projection? _____

6. Would the Prime Meridian and the equator be the same length on the interrupted projection? _____

Great Circle Routes

On a flat map, it looks like the shortest way from New York to Tokyo is to fly right over the Pacific Ocean. But if you look at a globe, you can see the shortest route goes way up north over Alaska.

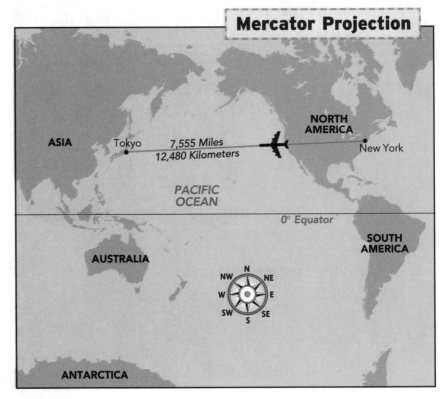

Mercator Projection

ASIA

Tokyo

7,555 Miles
12,480 Kilometers

NORTH AMERICA

New York

PACIFIC OCEAN

0° Equator

AUSTRALIA

SOUTH AMERICA

ANTARCTICA

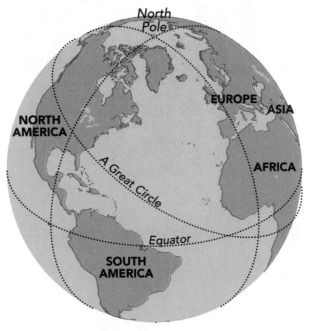

North Pole

EUROPE
ASIA

NORTH AMERICA

AFRICA

A Great Circle

Equator

SOUTH AMERICA

O n a map, the shortest distance between two points is a straight line. But on a globe, the shortest distance between two points is a segment or arc along a great circle. These arcs are called **great circle routes**. Navigators use them to plot the shortest air routes between two places. Airplanes save time and fuel by following great circle routes.

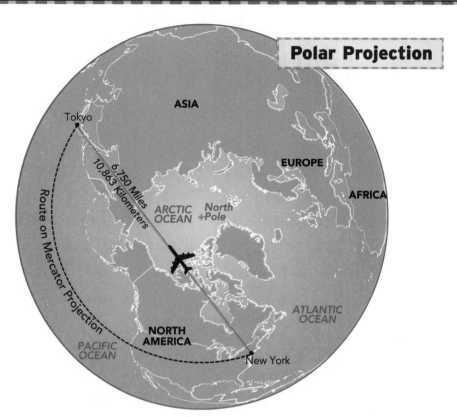

Polar Projection

ASIA

Tokyo

EUROPE

AFRICA

6,750 Miles
10,863 Kilometers

Route on Mercator Projection

ARCTIC OCEAN

North +Pole

ATLANTIC OCEAN

NORTH AMERICA

PACIFIC OCEAN

New York

MAP READER'S TIP

Stretch a rubber band around the center of a ball. You have made a great circle. With a marker, make two dots a little ways apart on the rubber band. You have marked off a great circle route.

Use the maps to answer these questions.

1. In which direction is the plane flying on the Mercator projection?_____

2. How many miles is the trip from New York
   to Tokyo on the Mercator projection? _____
   How many miles is it on the polar projection? _____
   How many miles can a pilot save?_____

3. What kind of route is the plane taking on the polar projection?_____

4. On the Mercator projection, what continent
   does the flight pass over?_____
   What continents does the route
   go over on the polar projection? _____

5. On the polar projection, what oceans does the plane fly over?_____
   What ocean does the plane fly
   over on the Mercator projection?_____

Using a Grid and Index

Some maps have a grid pattern over them to help you locate places more easily. The squares formed by a grid are marked with letters and numbers along the top, bottom, and sides of a map. The first square in the upper left corner of this map is A1. The square to the right of it is B1. What is the square just below A1?

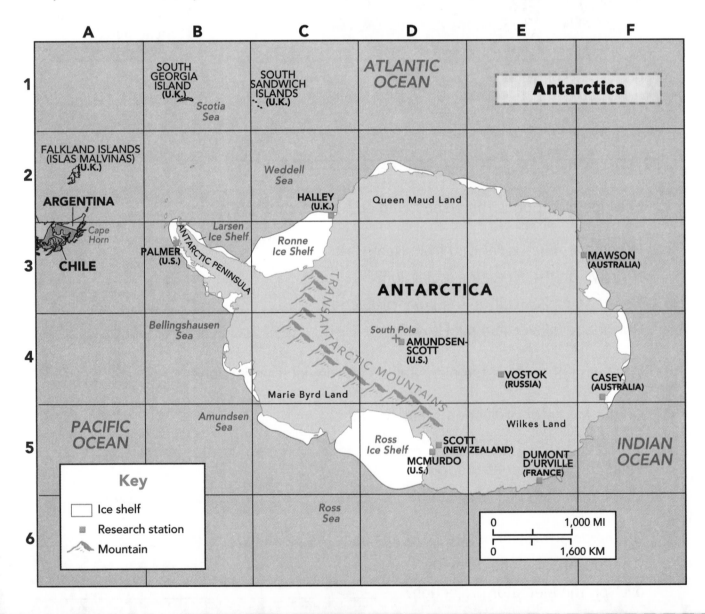

Use the map grid to answer these questions.

1. In which grid square is the South Pole?_____

2. What research station is in F4? _____

3. In which grid squares do you find the Transantarctic Mountains? _____

4. What sea is in C2? _____

5. Name three squares in which you find islands. _____

Maps often have an index to help you locate places. A map index is an alphabetical listing of places and the grid squares in which they are found.

Index		
Amundsen-Scott Station D4	McMurdo Station D5
Casey Station F4	Palmer Station B3
Dumont d'Urville Station E5	Scott Station D5
Halley Station C2	South Pole D4
Mawson Station F3	Vostok Station E4

6. You are working at the Palmer Research Station.
   What is your grid location? _____

7. What is the grid location of Halley Station? _____

8. What two stations are located in D5? _____

9. What place is listed after the South Pole on the index? _____

10. You are looking for the Casey Research Station on the index.
    Between what two listings will you find it? _____

Latitude and Longitude

Suppose you had a blue ball with a small red X on it. Could you describe the location of this X? Without any other markings on the ball, your task would be almost impossible. Long ago, geographers also found it difficult to describe the location of places on Earth.

L ines that run around Earth in an east-west direction are called lines of **latitude** or parallels. Parallel lines are all the same distance apart from one another; they never meet. These lines are measured in degrees, shown by the symbol °. The best-known parallel, the equator, is 0°. Parallels north of the equator are marked in degrees north (N), and parallels south of the equator are marked in degrees south (S).

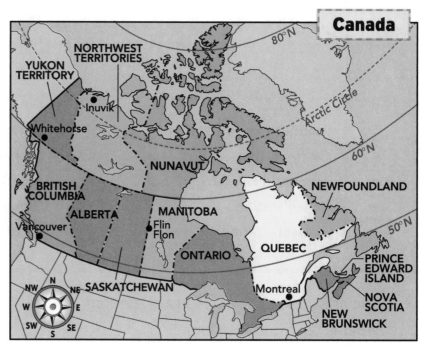

Canada

1. At about what degree of latitude is Vancouver?_____

2. Name a city that is north of the Arctic Circle. _____

3. Is most of Canada above or below the Arctic Circle? _____

4. What city is at about 55°N? _____

5. What parallel forms the northern border of four Canadian provinces? _____

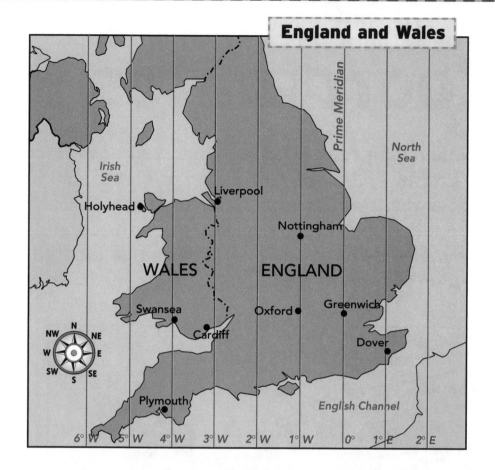

England and Wales

MAP READER'S TIP

Besides the equator, other important parallels are the Tropic of Cancer and the Tropic of Capricorn. The area between these is called the tropics. Two other parallels with special names are the Arctic Circle and the Antarctic Circle.

Lines that run north to south are called lines of **longitude** or meridians. The Prime Meridian is 0°. Meridians to the east of it are measured in degrees east (E), and meridians to the west of it are measured in degrees west (W). From the Prime Meridian to 180° longitude is exactly halfway around Earth. The line at 180° is called the International Dateline.

Unlike parallels, meridians are not all the same distance apart from one another. Instead, meridians come together at the North and South poles. They are farthest apart at the equator.

Use the lines of longitude to answer these questions.

6. What city is on the Prime Meridian?_____

7. Name a city in the east longitudes. _____

8. A city in Wales at about 4°W is _____ .
   An English city at about the same longitude is _____ .

9. About how many degrees of longitude do
   England and Wales cover altogether? _____

10. What is the longitude of Nottingham?_____

Map Coordinates

When you put latitude and longitude lines together, you have a grid. You can use the grid to find places on a map or globe. For example, the **coordinates** for New Orleans, Louisiana, are 30°N (latitude) and 90°W (longitude). Coordinates are the latitude and longitude address of a place. Every place on Earth can be located using this grid—even your own backyard!

1. If you are at 30°N, 95°W, what city are you in? _____

2. If you are at 25°N, 80°W, what city are you in? _____

3. The coordinates for Memphis are _____ .

4. What city is at about 48°N, 122°W? _____

5. What are the coordinates for New York City? _____

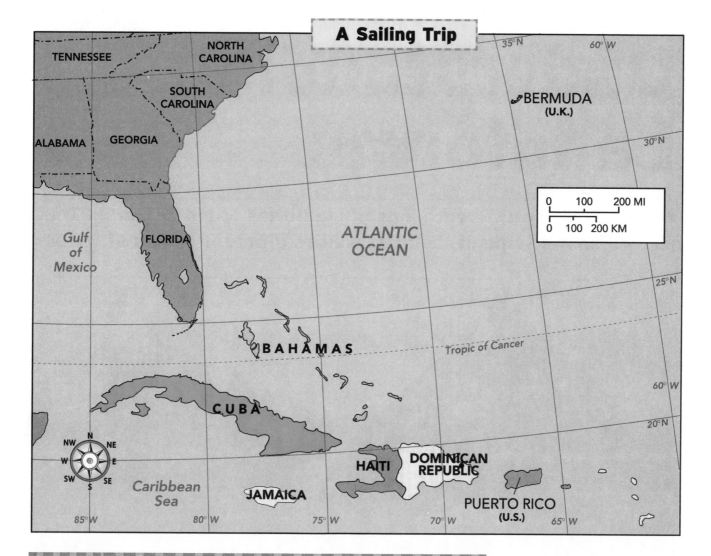

A Sailing Trip

Sailors often use latitude and longitude coordinates to plot a route. Use the coordinates on this chart to plot a sailing trip in the Atlantic Ocean and Caribbean Sea.

chart

Date	Latitude	Longitude
July 2	35°N	77°W
July 3	32°N	80°W
July 4	30°N	80°W
July 5	27°N	78°W
July 6	23°N	75°W
July 7	20°N	70°W
July 8	18°N	67°W

MAP READER'S TIP

To find even more precise locations on a global grid, each degree is divided into 60 minutes and each minute is divided into 60 seconds.

Understanding Landforms

There are many different kinds of landforms found on Earth. This picture shows some of them, as well as different bodies of water.

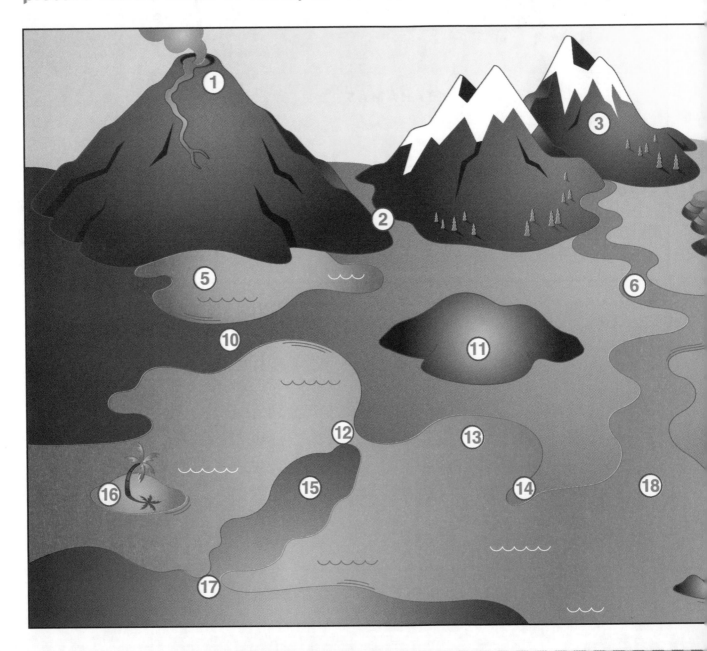

Can you match each description to the correct body of water or landform in the picture? Write the correct number on each line.

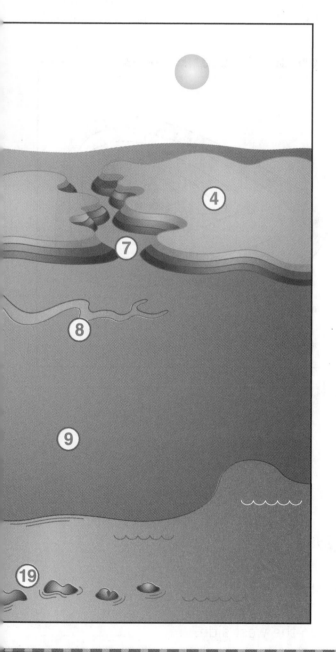

_____ An **archipelago** is a chain of islands.

_____ A **bay** is a small body of water partly enclosed by land.

_____ A **canyon** is a deep, narrow valley with high, steep sides.

_____ A **cape** is a narrow point of land that extends out into a body of water.

_____ A **gulf** is an arm of an ocean or sea that is partly enclosed by land.

_____ A **hill** is land that is higher than a plain but not as high or steep as a mountain.

_____ An **island** is land that is surrounded on all sides by water.

_____ An **isthmus** is a narrow strip of land that connects two large areas of land.

_____ A **lake** is a body of water entirely surrounded by land.

_____ A **mountain** is high, steep rugged land that rises sharply from the surrounding area.

_____ The **mouth of a river** is the place where a river empties into a larger body of water.

_____ A **peninsula** is an area of land that is surrounded by water on three sides.

_____ A **plain** is a broad area of open, flat land.

_____ A **plateau** is a large area of high, flat land.

_____ A **river** is a large stream of water that flows from higher land to lower land.

_____ A **strait** is a narrow channel that connects two larger bodies of water.

_____ A **tributary** is a small river or stream that flows into a larger river.

_____ A **valley** is the land that lies between mountains or hills.

_____ A **volcano** is a cone-shaped mountain that is formed by lava erupting from a crack in the Earth's surface.

Looking at Elevation

Geographers measure the height, or **elevation**, of land from sea level. **Sea level** is the average height of the ocean's surface. It is where the ocean meets the shore. Sea level is at zero elevation.

O n this page you can see two different views of Belle Island. The **profile** shows the island's side view. The **contour map** shows how the island looks from above. When the lines on a contour map are close together, they show that the land is steep. Lines farther apart show a more gradual incline.

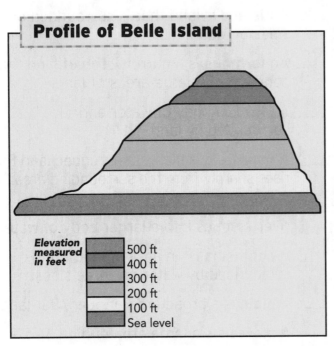

Profile of Belle Island

Elevation measured in feet
- 500 ft
- 400 ft
- 300 ft
- 200 ft
- 100 ft
- Sea level

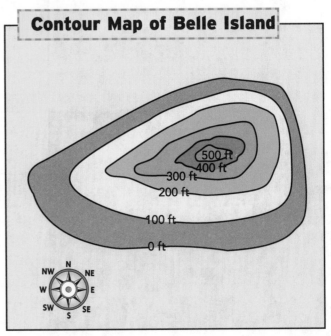

Contour Map of Belle Island

500 ft
400 ft
300 ft
200 ft
100 ft
0 ft

Use the maps to answer these questions.

1. What elevation does green represent on both the profile and the contour map? _____

2. What is the highest elevation of Belle Island? _____

3. Is the island steeper on the east or west side? _____

4. What color represents an elevation of 300 feet? _____

5. Why do you think the island's biggest town is on the west side? _____

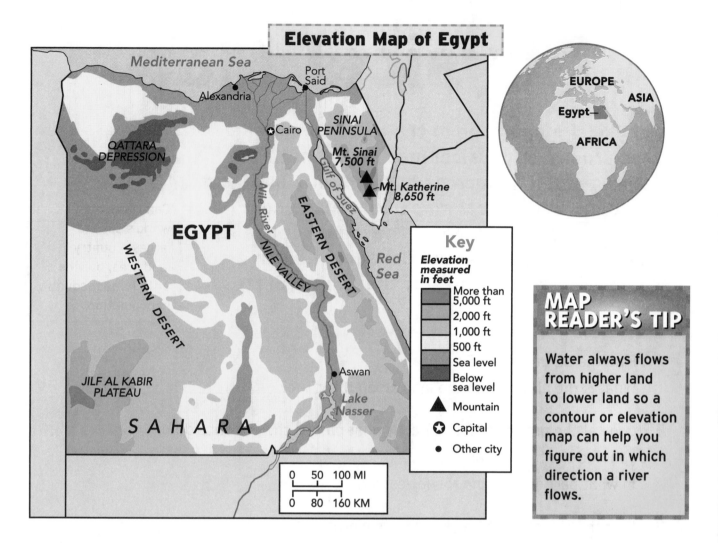

Elevation Map of Egypt

Mediterranean Sea

Alexandria · Port Said

☆ Cairo

QATTARA DEPRESSION

SINAI PENINSULA

Mt. Sinai 7,500 ft

▲ Mt. Katherine 8,650 ft

EGYPT

Nile River

EASTERN DESERT

Gulf of Suez

WESTERN DESERT

NILE VALLEY

Red Sea

JILF AL KABIR PLATEAU

· Aswan

Lake Nasser

S A H A R A

0   50   100 MI
0   80   160 KM

EUROPE

ASIA

Egypt—

AFRICA

Key

Elevation measured in feet

More than 5,000 ft
2,000 ft
1,000 ft
500 ft
Sea level
Below sea level

▲ Mountain
☆ Capital
· Other city

MAP READER'S TIP

Water always flows from higher land to lower land so a contour or elevation map can help you figure out in which direction a river flows.

This map shows the elevations of land in Egypt.
Use the map and its legend to answer these questions.

1. At what elevation is the land along the Mediterranean coast? _____

2. Find Egypt's largest area of land below sea level. What is it called? _____

3. In which part of Egypt is the land above 5,000 feet? _____

4. What is the elevation of most of the Western Desert? _____

5. In general, is Egypt's land higher in the north or south? _____

6. Most of the land around the Nile River and its valley is higher in the southern part than in the northern part. In which direction do you think the Nile flows? _____

sout west no outh eas t north east we th south
th
east we
st north
est west n
th sou
rth sou
rth sou
east w
h east

A Physical Map

A **physical map** is one of the most common maps around. A physical map shows natural features of Earth such as lakes, rivers, and land elevations. A physical map might also show cities, towns, and borders. The map on page 21 shows the eastern part of Canada. You can also see parts of some states of the United States.

MAP READER'S TIP

Canada is the world's second-largest country in land area, but the 34th largest country in population.

1. Find the St. Lawrence River.
    What is the elevation of the land along this river? _____

2. Look at the province of Ontario. In what part of the province do
    you find the highest land? _____
    In what part do you find the lowest land? _____

3. Find the city of Montreal. What is its elevation? _____
    Is it higher or lower than the city of Schefferville? _____

4. Locate Prince Edward Island. What is its elevation? _____

5. Into what body of water does the La Grande River flow? _____

6. In which direction does the Severn River flow? _____

7. If you drove directly west from Halifax,
    how would the elevation change? _____

8. The Laurentian Mountains are found in Quebec.
    In what part of this province would you expect them to be? _____

9. What is the elevation along the border between Minnesota and Ontario? _____

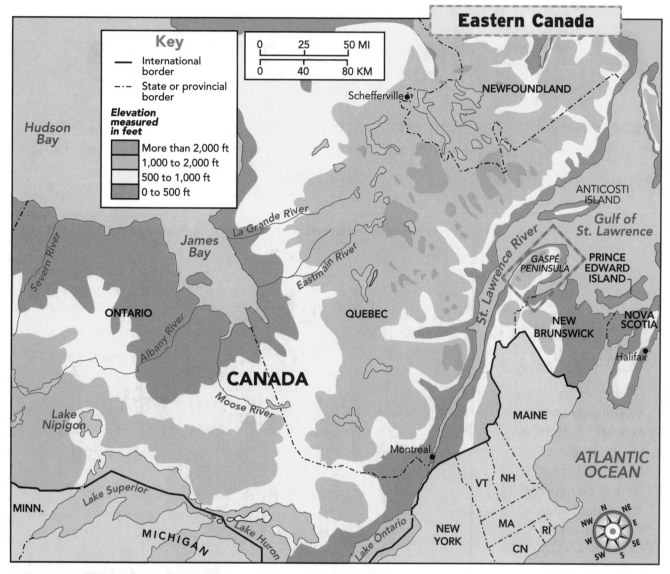

Eastern Canada

Key

— International border

-·- State or provincial border

Elevation measured in feet

More than 2,000 ft
1,000 to 2,000 ft
500 to 1,000 ft
0 to 500 ft

0   25   50 MI
0   40   80 KM

Hudson Bay

NEWFOUNDLAND

Schefferville

ANTICOSTI ISLAND

Gulf of St. Lawrence

La Grande River

James Bay

Eastmain River

GASPÉ PENINSULA

PRINCE EDWARD ISLAND

St. Lawrence River

Severn River

ONTARIO

Albany River

QUEBEC

NEW BRUNSWICK

NOVA SCOTIA

Halifax

CANADA

Moose River

MAINE

ATLANTIC OCEAN

Lake Nipigon

Montreal

VT   NH

MINN.

Lake Superior

Lake Huron

MICHIGAN

NEW YORK

MA   RI

CN

Lake Ontario

N NE E SE S SW W NW

BONUS QUESTIONS

Use the map and profile to answer the bonus questions.

1. Which part of the Gaspé Peninsula is steepest? _____

2. Which part of the Gaspé Peninsula is probably easiest to cross? _____

   Why? _____

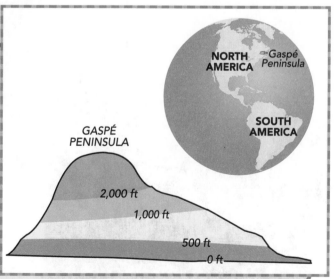

NORTH AMERICA — Gaspé Peninsula

SOUTH AMERICA

GASPÉ PENINSULA

2,000 ft
1,000 ft
500 ft
0 ft

A Land Use Map

People use Earth's land and water in many ways. The map on this page is a **land use map** of India. A land use map shows how people use the land to produce income.

MAP READER'S TIP

Much of India forms a peninsula that extends south from the continent of Asia. The land of India is sometimes called the Indian subcontinent.

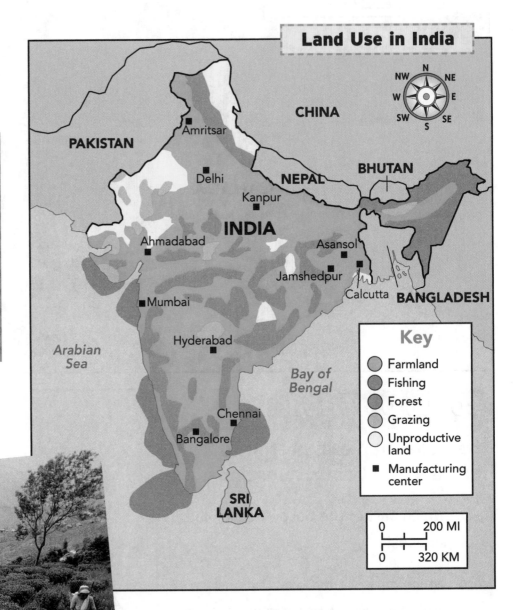

Land Use in India

CHINA

PAKISTAN

Amritsar

Delhi

Kanpur

NEPAL

BHUTAN

INDIA

Ahmadabad

Asansol

Jamshedpur

Mumbai

Calcutta   BANGLADESH

Hyderabad

Arabian Sea

Bay of Bengal

Chennai

Bangalore

SRI LANKA

Key
- Farmland
- Fishing
- Forest
- Grazing
- Unproductive land
- ■ Manufacturing center

| 0 | 200 MI |
| 0 | 320 KM |

India is the world's largest producer of tea. India's warm climate is perfect for growing this crop.

Circle the best answer for each question.

1. Most of the land in India is used for _____.

   a. grazing   b. manufacturing   c. farming

2. Fishing is a way of life for people along _____ of India's coastline.

   a. all   b. some   c. little

3. Most of India's goats and sheep probably graze in the _____ part of the country.

   a. southern   b. central   c. northwestern

4. Two southern manufacturing centers are _____ and _____.

   a. Kanpur and Jamshedpur   b. Bangalore and Chennai   c. Amritsar and Delhi

5. The land surrounding Calcutta is used for _____.

   a. grazing   b. farming   c. forestry

6. Cotton grown in India is made into cloth in large textile mills.
   A city on the Arabian Sea with many cotton mills would be _____.

   a. Chennai   b. Ahmadabad   c. Mumbai

7. India has two large areas of unproductive land.
   This land might be _____.

   a. mountains and deserts   b. hills and valleys   c. plains and forests

WORD SCRAMBLE

Can you unscramble the names of five manufacturing centers in India?

ATCAUTCL   MDADBAHAA   PRASUEHJMD   DYDAABREH   TARMIASR

_____   _____   _____   _____   _____

Comparing Maps

Bright colored leaves are a sure sign of autumn. In the northeastern part of the United States, the fall foliage is often spectacular.

The maps on these pages show when the leaves turn color in the Northeast. The term "peak" means that the color of the leaves is at its best. The difference between these two maps is just one week. By comparing these maps you can follow the changing foliage.

MAP READER'S TIP

Six of the states on this map are part of a region known as New England. These states are Maine, New Hampshire, Vermont, Massachusetts, Connecticut, and Rhode Island.

Foliage: First Week in October

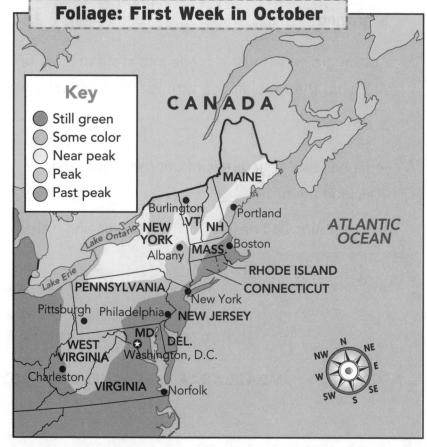

Key
- Still green
- Some color
- Near peak
- Peak
- Past peak

CANADA

MAINE

Burlington
Portland

NEW YORK
VT
NH

Lake Ontario

Albany
Boston
MASS.

Lake Erie

RHODE ISLAND

PENNSYLVANIA
CONNECTICUT

New York

Pittsburgh
Philadelphia
NEW JERSEY

MD.
DEL.

WEST VIRGINIA
Washington, D.C.

Charleston

VIRGINIA
Norfolk

ATLANTIC OCEAN

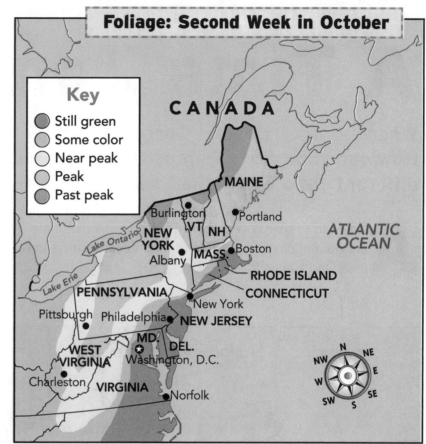

Foliage: Second Week in October

Key
- Still green
- Some color
- Near peak
- Peak
- Past peak

CANADA

MAINE

Burlington
Portland

VT NH

Lake Ontario

NEW YORK
Albany

MASS. Boston

RHODE ISLAND
CONNECTICUT

Lake Erie

PENNSYLVANIA

New York

Pittsburgh Philadelphia

NEW JERSEY

MD.
WEST VIRGINIA
Washington, D.C.

DEL.

Charleston VIRGINIA

Norfolk

ATLANTIC OCEAN

1. By the second week in October, would you see any fall colors in Norfolk, Virginia? _____
In which part of Virginia would you see colorful leaves?

_____

2. During the first week of October, where would the leaves be at their peak? _____

3. What happens to that same region by the second week in October? _____

4. Find Portland on both maps. How do the leaves change there in one week? _____

5. Suppose you were in Pittsburgh on October 2.
What would the leaves be like? _____

6. By the third week in October, what would you expect the leaves
to be like in Albany? _____ In Washington, D.C.? _____

7. You are going to travel for a few weeks in the Northeast. You want to see as much
fall foliage as you can. Where would you start your trip? _____
Where would you end it? _____

8. Find the areas on the second map where the leaves are past peak.
Describe how the trees would look there. _____

A Time Zone Map

When it's six o'clock in Georgia, it's only five o'clock in Oklahoma. How can it be two different times at once? Earth is divided into different time zones that are one hour apart.

Asingle time zone covers about 15 degrees of longitude. There are 24 time zones in all, so at every hour of the day, it is a different time in each time zone. This map shows the four time zones of the mainland United States.

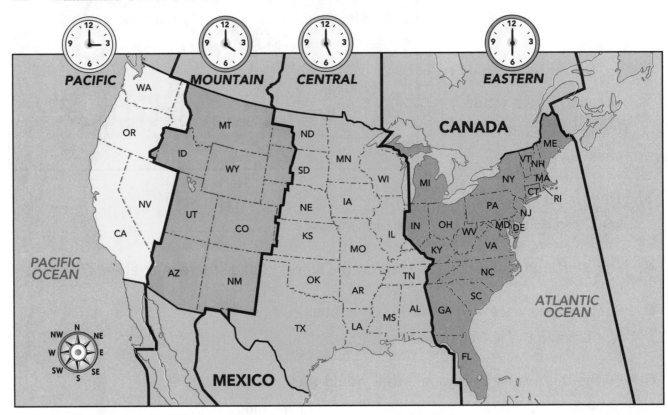

1. When it is 4 p.m. in New Mexico, it is _____ in Nevada.

2. You watch a baseball game on television that starts in Ohio at 2 p.m.
   What time does the game start in southern Idaho? _____

3. In which time zone is Oregon? _____ Rhode Island? _____ Alabama? _____

4. Julie lives in eastern Nebraska, and Sidney lives in
   western South Dakota. Are they in the same time zone? _____

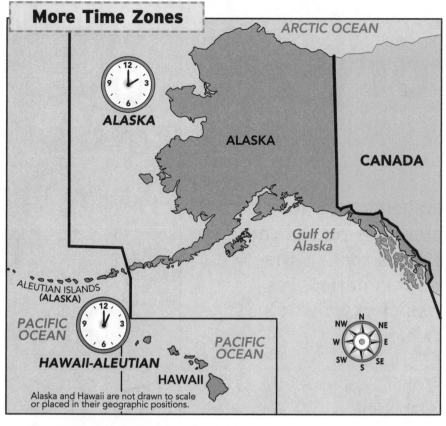

More Time Zones

ARCTIC OCEAN

ALASKA

ALASKA

CANADA

Gulf of Alaska

ALEUTIAN ISLANDS (ALASKA)

PACIFIC OCEAN

HAWAII-ALEUTIAN

HAWAII

PACIFIC OCEAN

Alaska and Hawaii are not drawn to scale or placed in their geographic positions.

MAP READER'S TIP

Earth makes a complete rotation every 24 hours. As Earth turns, part of it receives sunlight, and a new day begins there. At the same time, another part of Earth darkens, and night begins there. When it is noon on one side of Earth, it is midnight on the opposite side.

Alaska and Hawaii are in different time zones than the rest of the U.S. Most of Alaska is one time zone west of California. However, part of Alaska—the Aleutian Islands—is in the next time zone west. This is the same time zone as Hawaii.

5. How many hours difference is there in time between Delaware and Hawaii? _____

6. Emma lives in Maine. She is going to call three friends at 10 a.m. her local time. Toni lives in Iowa, Brandon lives in Arizona, and Peggy lives in South Carolina. What time will the call come through for each friend?

Toni _____   Brandon _____   Peggy _____

7. A store in Hawaii gets a call from a customer in California at 2 p.m. What time is it in California? _____

8. Imagine that you are in Vermont. It is 7 a.m. and you are waking up. Your friend lives in Wyoming. What is your friend most likely doing at this time? _____

A History Map

Maps can show historical events. The map on these pages shows the routes that different European explorers took in the 1400s and early 1500s. This period was one of the greatest times of exploration the world has ever known.

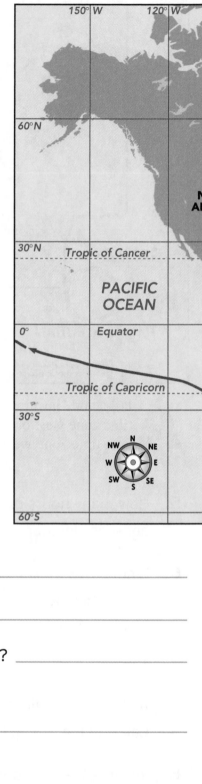

1. Which explorer left from Bristol? _____
   Where did his explorations take him? _____

2. What color is the route for Christopher Columbus?
   _____
   What island did he reach on his voyage? _____

3. Which explorer is represented by a green arrow?
   _____
   From what European city did he begin his voyage? _____

4. What two continents did Vasco da Gama sail to? _____

5. Where was the first place that Ferdinand Magellan stopped? _____

6. About how many years after Columbus
   made his voyages did Magellan set sail? _____

7. Where did Magellan have to sail to get
   from the Atlantic Ocean to the Pacific Ocean? _____
   What body of water is named for this explorer? _____

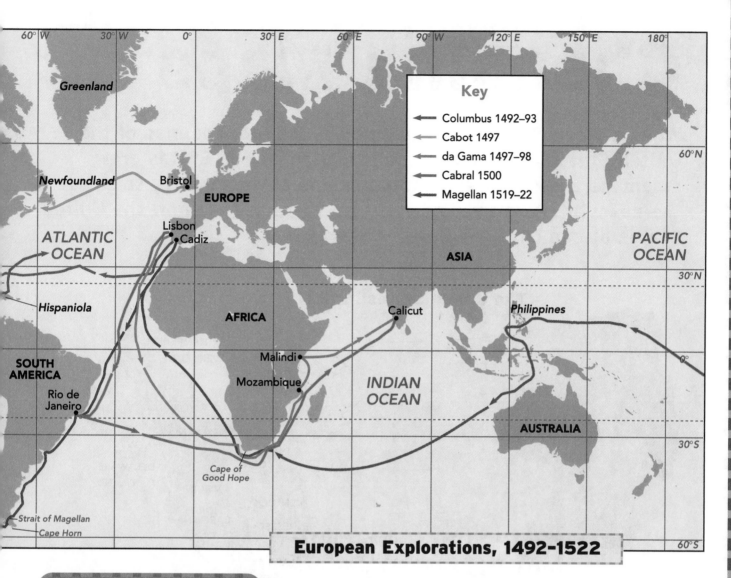

European Explorations, 1492–1522

Key
- ← Columbus 1492–93
- ← Cabot 1497
- ← da Gama 1497–98
- ← Cabral 1500
- ← Magellan 1519–22

WORD SEARCH

Can you find the names of five European explorers?

```
N O C P Z A Y T L
A D A G A M A Q N
S U B M U L O C I
U J O G P K L A M
H E T I U O M B O
V Y X R A B K R A
R N A L L E G A M
W I H O K A B L S
```

MAP READER'S TIP

America was named for an Italian, Amerigo Vespucci, who explored the New World between 1497 and 1503.

Changing Maps

When a place changes, then maps change too. The map of the United States is a good example. As the United States grew, mapmakers had to keep changing maps of the country to show the new state borders. The maps on these pages show the United States at two different times in the past.

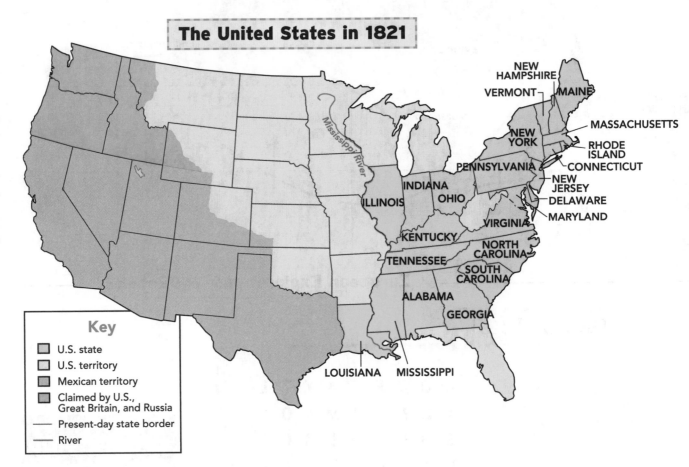

The United States in 1821

Key
- ☐ U.S. state
- ☐ U.S. territory
- ☐ Mexican territory
- ☐ Claimed by U.S., Great Britain, and Russia
- — Present-day state border
- — River

Use the maps to answer these questions.

1. How many states were there in 1821? _____ In 1861? _____

2. Find the Mississippi River. In 1821 were most of the states east or west of this river? _____

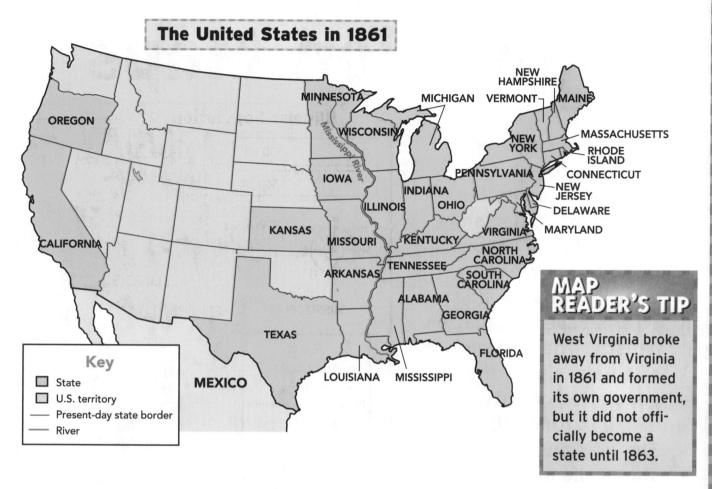

The United States in 1861

Key
- State
- U.S. territory
- — Present-day state border
- — River

MAP READER'S TIP

West Virginia broke away from Virginia in 1861 and formed its own government, but it did not officially become a state until 1863.

How many states were west of the Mississippi in 1861? _____

3. What country owned most of the land in the west in 1821? _____

4. What country lost the most land to the U.S. between 1821 and 1861? _____

5. Was California a state in 1821? _____ Was it a state in 1861? _____

6. Name three states that joined the
   nation between 1821 and 1861. _____

7. What color on the map key represents your state in 1821? _____
   What color represents your state in 1861? _____

8. How would you expect the map of the United
   States to change by the end of the 1800s? _____

Population Maps

The number of people living in a place is called the **population**. A population map shows the number of people living in a certain area, usually a square mile. This is called population density. The map on this page shows the population density of the state of Illinois. The map on page 33 shows the population density of South Carolina.

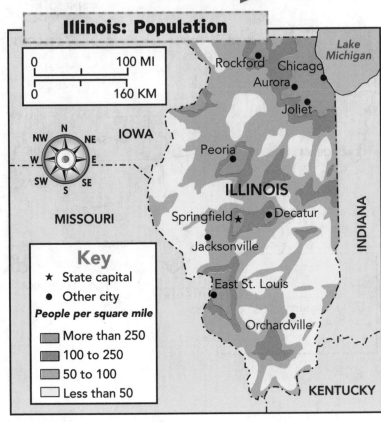

Illinois: Population

0	100 MI
0	160 KM

IOWA

MISSOURI

ILLINOIS

INDIANA

KENTUCKY

Lake Michigan

Rockford · Chicago
Aurora ·
· Joliet
· Peoria
Springfield ★ · Decatur
· Jacksonville
· East St. Louis
· Orchardville

Key
★ State capital
● Other city
People per square mile
▢ More than 250
▢ 100 to 250
▢ 50 to 100
▢ Less than 50

Use the maps to answer the questions.

1. Where is the greatest population density in Illinois? _____
   Where is the second greatest density? _____

2. About how many people live in a square mile in Jacksonville? _____

3. Name a city in Illinois with a population density of less
   than 50 people per square mile. _____

4. How would you describe Illinois' population in
   the southeastern part of the state? _____

5. How might Lake Michigan have helped Chicago's population grow? _____

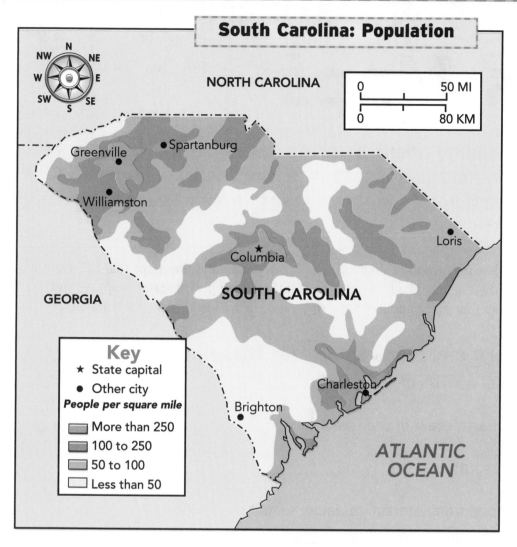

South Carolina: Population

NORTH CAROLINA

0 ——————— 50 MI
0 ——————— 80 KM

Greenville
Spartanburg
Williamston

GEORGIA

Columbia

SOUTH CAROLINA

Loris

Key
- ★ State capital
- ● Other city

People per square mile
- More than 250
- 100 to 250
- 50 to 100
- Less than 50

Charleston

Brighton

ATLANTIC OCEAN

MAP READER'S TIP

Illinois is the sixth largest state in population, and South Carolina is the 25th largest.

6. Around what cities is South Carolina's population greatest? _____

_____

7. In which population category is Williamston? _____ Loris? _____

8. Would you describe the population in the southwestern part of the state as high or low? _____

9. Which of these are not shown on the map: _____
   a. total state population
   b. the most densely populated cities
   c. where the most farmers live

10. What are the advantages of living in a highly populated area? _____
   What are the disadvantages? _____

News Maps

Suppose you're reading about a current event in the country of Japan. A map can help you locate it. News occurs all over the world, and news articles often have maps to help readers identify where these events take place.

O n page 35 is the first paragraph of a news story about Japan and the maps that illustrate it. The large map shows Japan. The smaller map is an **inset map**, or locator map. An inset map is a small map that gives another view of a place. This inset map shows Japan's location in the world.

Use the news story and maps to answer these questions.

1. Japan is made up of a series of _____ .

2. Zentsuji is on the north coast of the island of _____ .

3. The body of water south of Japan is the _____ .

4. Melons being shipped from Zentsuji to Japan's capital
   would travel in which direction? _____

5. Melons that are exported northwest from
   Zentsuji would go to which country? _____ .

WORD SCRAMBLE

Can you unscramble the names of the four main islands of Japan?

UHOSNH _____

HYUSKU _____

IKDOHKOA _____

IHKSKUO _____

Shaping Up Melons

In Japan the geometry of melons is changing. Farmers in Zentsuji on the island of Shikoku thought their melons needed shaping up. Their plump round watermelons were tasty, but they rolled around in refrigerators. So the Zentsuji farmers began reshaping their fruit. They now place square glass cases on the melons when the fruit is still small on the vine. As a result, the melons grow square in shape. They fit better in refrigerators and are easier to carry.

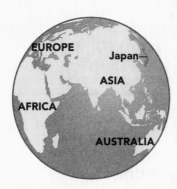

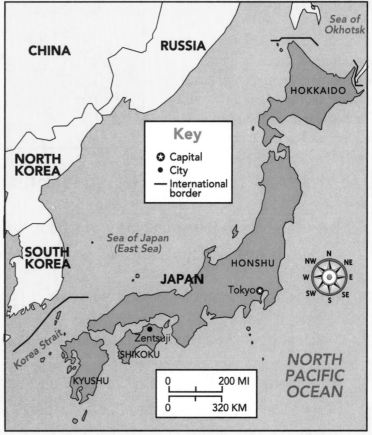

Literature Maps

When you read a book, do you notice the setting? Often, fictional stories are set in real places. The maps on these pages show where two well-known books take place.

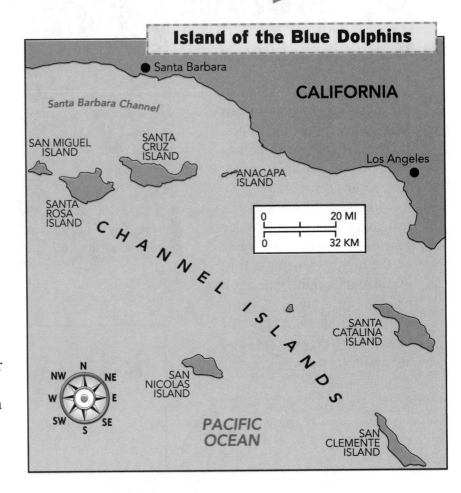

Island of the Blue Dolphins

sland of the Blue Dolphins by Scott O'Dell is about a girl named Karana who lives with her family and tribe on an island in the Pacific Ocean. After her family is killed in a battle with hunters from a ship, Karana remains on the island by herself. The book tells of the many challenges Karana faces.

Use the map to answer the questions.

1. The Island of the Blue Dolphins in the book is San Nicolas Island. Circle this island on the map, then draw a dolphin in the sea near it.

2. What island is southeast of San Nicolas? _____

3. Which state do you think the Channel Islands are part of? _____

4. After many years Karana goes to the Santa Barbara Mission. Draw a line from her island to Santa Barbara. In which direction does Karana travel?_____

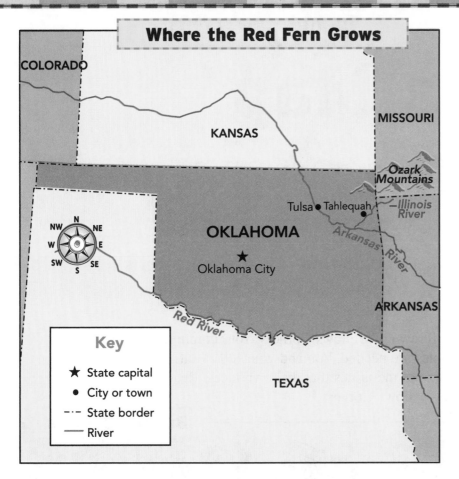

Where the Red Fern Grows

COLORADO

KANSAS

MISSOURI

Ozark Mountains

Tulsa ● Tahlequah

Illinois River

OKLAHOMA

Arkansas River

★ Oklahoma City

ARKANSAS

Red River

TEXAS

Key

★ State capital
● City or town
-·-· State border
—— River

MAP READER'S TIP

When you read books set in real places, locate these places on a map to get a better idea of where they are. Some other books with real-place settings are: *Number the Stars* by Lois Lowry, *The Cay* by Theodore Taylor, *Shiloh* by Phyllis Reynolds Naylor, *Caddie Woodlawn* by Carol Ryrie Brink, and *The View from Saturday* by E.L. Konigsberg.

The map on this page shows the real-life location for another book of fiction. This book, by Wilson Rawls, is called *Where the Red Fern Grows*. It's a story about a boy named Billy Colman and his two beloved hounds, Little Ann and Old Dan. The book recounts Billy's adventures and triumphs with his amazing dogs.

Use the map to answer these questions.

5. In the story Billy walks 20 miles to pick up his hounds at the depot in Tahlequah. In which part of Oklahoma is Tahlequah? _____

6. Billy and his family live in the Ozarks of Oklahoma. What landform do they live near? _____

7. Billy and his dogs do much of their hunting along a river. What is the river nearest to Tahlequah? _____

8. What other states are close to Billy's home? _____

9. In which direction is the capital of Oklahoma from Billy's home? _____

Using a Map to Plan

You can use a map to make plans and decisions. For example, most people use maps when planning a vacation or business trip. Maps can also be useful when planning for the future.

Imagine that you live in the small town of Bellows Corners. Your community is growing. As more people move in, more homes are needed. You and your fellow citizens want to plan the town's growth. Page 39 lists some of the issues that the town faces. Read the questions and study the map to help the people of Bellows Corners.

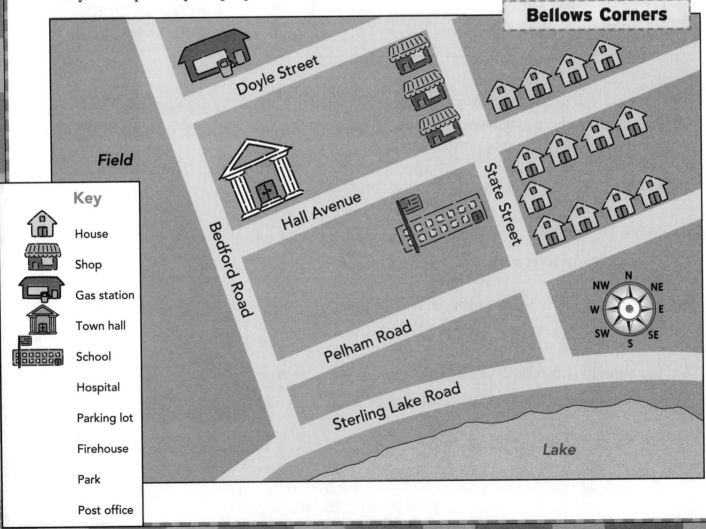

Bellows Corners

Field

Key

- House
- Shop
- Gas station
- Town hall
- School
- Hospital
- Parking lot
- Firehouse
- Park
- Post office

Doyle Street

Hall Avenue

Bedford Road

State Street

Pelham Road

Sterling Lake Road

Lake

NW N NE
W E
SW S SE

Use the map to answer these questions.

1. Bellows Corners is now laid out in a grid pattern.

   Why do you think city planners use this pattern? _____

   _____

2. The post office for Bellows Corners is currently in the back of a store.

   A new building is needed. Where should it go? Draw it in the key and on the map.

3. A big company wants to build a factory by the lake.

   How might a factory help Bellows Corners? _____

   How might it hurt the town? _____

   What would your decision be? _____

4. A builder wants to put up an apartment complex in the field.

   Would this be a good use of the land? _____

   What is another possible use for this land? _____

5. A developer wants to build a shopping mall the entire length of Doyle Street.

   He would tear down the gas station to make way for the mall.

   What do you think of this idea? _____

   Why? _____

6. Here is a list of other needs in Bellows Corners. Create a symbol for
   each one in the key and then draw it on the map.

   hospital   parking lot

   firehouse   park

MAP READER'S TIP

One of the first people to plan a city based on a grid pattern was Hippodamus. Thousands of years ago, he designed a city in Greece called Miletus.

7. What else would you plan for Bellows Corners?

   _____

   _____

   Where would you put it? _____

A Map Challenge

Instead of labels, this United States map has numbers. Your challenge is to use the clues on the next page to identify each numbered place on the map. You may need to use other maps, encyclopedias, or your social studies textbook.

MAP READER'S TIP

The United States is the world's fourth largest country in size.

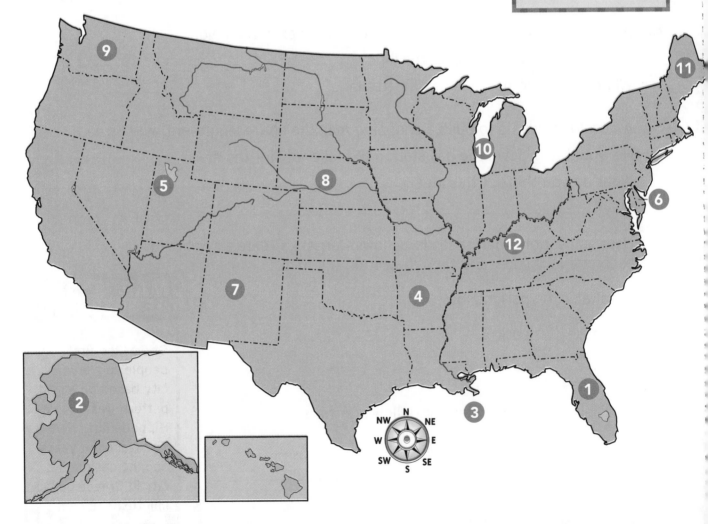

Write the name of each numbered state or body of water.

_____ 1. St. Augustine, the oldest permanent settlement of Europeans in the United States, is in this state.

_____ 2. The highest mountain in the U.S., Mt. McKinley, is in this state.

_____ 3. The Mississippi River flows into this body of water.

_____ 4. The capital of this state is Little Rock.

_____ 5. The Great Salt Lake, a body of water saltier than the oceans, is in this state.

_____ 6. This state was the first to approve the U.S. Constitution in 1787.

_____ 7. Pioneers and traders followed the Santa Fe Trail to what is now the capital of this state.

_____ 8. The Platte River runs from west to east across this state.

_____ 9. This state was named for the first President of the United States.

_____ 10. This is the only one of the Great Lakes that the United States does not share with Canada.

_____ 11. This state was once part of Massachusetts.

_____ 12. This state is bordered by seven other states including Virginia.

WORD SCRAMBLE

Can you unscramble these letters to spell the names of five states?

BAALMAA   **INTCEUCTCNO**   **GIHMCAIN**   **OOLADROC**   **SGTINNHAWO**

_____   _____   _____   _____   _____

Map Review 1

Use the map to answer the questions.

Mexico: Elevation

120 W CALIFORNIA 110 W NEW MEXICO UNITED STATES 100 W ALABAMA MISS. 90 W

Tijuana ARIZONA LOUISIANA FLORIDA

TEXAS 30 N

Rio Grande

BAJA CALIFORNIA Gulf of California SIERRA MADRE OCCIDENTAL Monterrey Matamoros Gulf of Mexico

Key

— International border

✪ Capital city

● City

Elevation measured in feet

More than 10,000 ft
5,000 to 10,000 ft
2,000 to 5,000 ft
1,000 to 2,000 ft
500 to 1,000 ft
0 to 500 ft

PACIFIC OCEAN Guadalajara SIERRA MADRE ORIENTAL MEXICO Tropic of Cancer

Campeche YUCATÁN PENINSULA 20 N

Mexico City Veracruz

0 ___ 200 MI
0 ___ 320 KM

Acapulco SIERRA MADRE DEL SUR BELIZE

GUATEMALA

1. What is the elevation of most of the Yucatán Peninsula? _____

2. What river forms the border between northeast Mexico and the United States? _____

3. What is the elevation of Mexico's capital city? _____

4. Find Baja California. What is the name for this landform? _____

5. Is Mexico in the northern or southern hemisphere? _____
   The Eastern or Western Hemisphere? _____

6. What is the longitude and latitude for Campeche? _____

7. What is the highest elevation of the Sierra Madre Mountains? _____

8. What city is at these coordinates: 21°N, 104°W? _____

Map Review 2

Use the map to answer the questions.

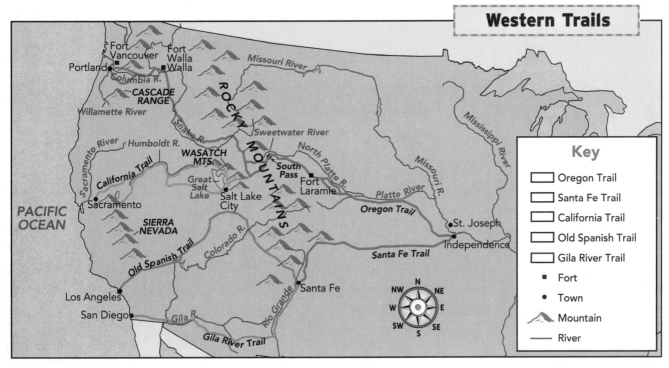

Western Trails

Key

☐ Oregon Trail
☐ Santa Fe Trail
☐ California Trail
☐ Old Spanish Trail
☐ Gila River Trail
■ Fort
● Town
⛰ Mountain
— River

1. Complete the map key by drawing in the correct color for the four trails.

2. You can tell that pioneers heading west left from _____ .

3. In which direction was the trail to Santa Fe? _____

4. To continue west from Santa Fe, a traveler could
   take either the _____ or the _____ .

5. The first river that travelers on the Oregon Trail had to cross was the _____ .

6. You can guess from the map labels that the elevation of the land _____
   as the pioneers moved west along the Oregon Trail.

7. From Salt Lake City, the California Trail led travelers around the _____ .

8. Write the name of the trail that ended at these places:
   Portland _____ San Diego _____ Sacramento _____

Thinking About Maps

Use what you have learned about maps
to complete the crossword puzzle.

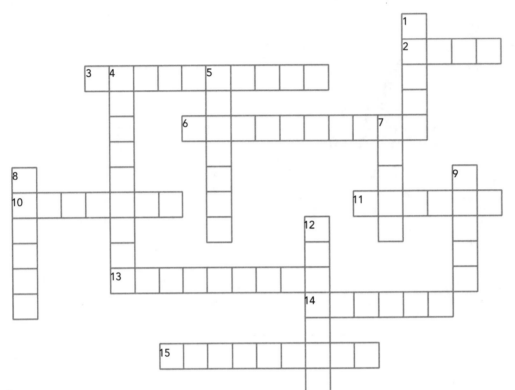

Across

2. imaginary line on which
   Earth rotates
3. half of the globe
6. the number of people
   in a place
10. the line that is 0° latitude
11. a deep, narrow valley
13. the direction between
   north and west
14. the most western state
   of the United States
15. Meridians are lines of
   _____.

Down

1. an island country in Asia
4. the height of land above
   sea level
5. the side view of the
   elevation of a place
7. a large body of water
8. the country that borders the
   United States to the south
9. The United States has
   six time _____.
12. a narrow strip of land that
   connects two large areas
   of land

Glossary

axis
An axis is an imaginary center line on which Earth turns.

archipelago
An archipelago is a chain of islands.

canyon
A canyon is a deep, narrow valley with high, steep sides.

cape
A cape is a narrow point of land that extends out into a body of water.

compass rose
A compass rose is a symbol that shows directions. The cardinal directions are north, south, east, and west. The intermediate directions are northeast, southeast, southwest, and northwest.

coordinates
Coordinates show the latitude and longitude of a place on a map.

contour map
A contour map has lines that show the elevations of different parts of land.

elevation
Elevation is the height of land measured from sea level.

equator
The equator is a line of latitude that runs around the center of Earth and divides it into the Northern and Southern hemispheres.

great circle routes
Great circle routes are arcs on circles that divide Earth in half. Navigators use these to plot the shortest distance between two places.

gulf
A gulf is an arm of an ocean or sea that is partly enclosed by land.

hemisphere
A hemisphere is half of Earth. Earth can be divided into the Northern and Southern hemispheres or the Eastern and Western hemispheres.

inset map
An inset map is a small map, also called a locator, that shows where a place is located.

isthmus
An isthmus is a narrow strip of land that connects two large areas of land.

land use map
A land use map shows how people use land to produce income.

latitude

Lines of latitude run east and west on a globe and are parallel to one another. These lines are also called parallels. The equator is a line of latitude.

longitude

Lines of longitude run between the North and South poles. These lines are also called meridians.

map legend

A map legend shows what symbols stand for. It is also called a map key.

meridian

A meridian is a line of longitude. The Prime Meridian is at 0 degrees.

mouth of river

The mouth of a river is the place where a river empties into a larger body of water.

peninsula

A peninsula is an area of land that is surrounded by water on three sides.

physical map

A physical map shows natural features of Earth such as lakes, rivers, and land elevations. A physical map can also show features such as cities, towns, and borders.

plateau

A plateau is a large area of high, flat land.

population map

A population map shows the density of people living in a place.

projections

Map projections are different ways of showing Earth on a flat sheet of paper.

scale

A map scale helps you measure distance on a map.

sea level

Sea level is the average height of the ocean's surface. It is 0 elevation.

strait

A strait is a narrow channel that connects two larger bodies of water.

time zone

A time zone covers about 15 degrees of longitude. There are 24 time zones on Earth.

tributary

A tributary is a small river or stream that flows into a larger river.

volcano

A volcano is a cone-shaped mountain that is formed by lava erupting from a crack in Earth's surface.

Answers

Page 3:
1. River walk; Milwaukee River
2. Lake Michigan; east
3. Pabst Mansion
4. about 1 mile
5. 94
6. west
7. Marcus Center for the Performing Arts
8. Possible answer: The harbor on the lake enabled the city to increase its trade which led to more business and growth.

Page 5:
1. Northern Hemisphere
2. equator
3. south
4. Southern and Eastern
5. South America
6. the 0° line of longitude
7. east and west

Page 7:
1. round
2. Mercator
3. Northern Hemisphere; Southern
4. polar projection
5. It's in four parts.
6. no

Page 9:
1. west
2. 7,755; 6,750; 1,005
3. great circle route
4. North America; North America; Asia
5. Arctic and Pacific; Pacific

Page 11:
1. D4
2. Casey
3. C3, C4, D4, D5
4. Weddell Sea
5. B1, B2, B3, C1, A2
6. B3
7. C2
8. McMurdo and Scott
9. Vostok Station
10. Amundsen-Scott and Dumont d'Urville

Pages 12–13:
1. 50°N
2. Inuvik
3. below
4. Flin Flon
5. 60°N
6. Greenwich
7. Dover
8. Swansea; Plymouth
9. 7-8 degrees
10. 1°W

Page 14:
1. Houston
2. Miami
3. 35°N, 90°W
4. Seattle
5. 41°N, 75°W

Page 15:
Check to see that students plot the route correctly.

Pages 16–17:
19, 13, 7, 14, 10, 11, 16, 17, 5, 3, 18, 15, 9, 4, 6, 12, 8, 2, 1

Page 18:
1. sea level to 100 feet
2. 500 feet
3. east
4. orange
5. The land isn't so steep there; it would be easier to build on.

Page 19:
1. at sea level
2. Qattara Depression
3. on the Sinai Peninsula and Jilf al Kabir Plateau
4. 1,000 to 2,000 feet
5. south
6. north

Pages 20–21:
1. sea level to 500 feet
2. southern; along Hudson Bay
3. sea level to 500 feet; lower
4. 0 to 500 feet
5. James Bay
6. north

7. It would be higher.
8. where the elevation is more than 2,000 feet
9. 1,000 to 2,000 feet

Bonus questions:
1. the western side
2. the eastern side; it is not as steep

Page 23:
1. c
2. b
3. c
4. b
5. b
6. c
7. a

Page 25:
1. no; western
2. northern parts of Maine, New Hampshire, Vermont, New York
3. Much of it is past peak.
4. They change from some color to peak.
5. some color
6. Possible answer: peak or past peak; some color or near peak
7. in the north near Canada; in southern Virginia
8. They would be almost bare.

Pages 26–27:
1. 3 o'clock
2. 12 o'clock
3. Pacific; Eastern; Central
4. no
5. 5
6. Toni: 9 a.m.
   Brandon: 8 a.m.
   Peggy: 10 a.m.
7. 4 p.m.
8. sleeping

Answers

Page 30:
1. Cabot; North America
2. blue; Hispaniola
3. Cabral; Lisbon
4. Africa; Asia
5. South America
6. about 27
7. around the southern tip of South America; the Strait of Magellan

Pages 30–31:
1. 23; 34
2. east; nine
3. Mexico
4. Mexico
5. no; yes
6. Possible answers: California, Oregon, Texas, Kansas, Arkansas, Minnesota, Michigan, Florida, Iowa, Wisconsin, Missouri
7. Answers will vary.
8. There would be more states in the territories.

Pages 32–33:
1. near the cities of Chicago and East St. Louis
2. from 50 to 100
3. Orchardville
4. less dense than the northeastern part
5. As a port on the lake, Chicago would have grown because of trade.
6. Charleston, Greenville, Columbia, Spartanburg
7. 100 to 250; 50 to 100
8. It's not very densely populated.
9. a and c
10. Possible answers: more cultural facilities, more businesses and jobs; crowding, traffic, noise.

Page 34:
1. islands
2. Shikoku
3. North Pacific Ocean
4. northeast
5. South Korea

Page 36–37:
1. Check to see that students follow directions.
2. San Clemente
3. California
4. north
5. northeast
6. Ozark Mountains
7. Illinois River
8. Missouri, Arkansas, Kansas
9. southwest

Page 39:
1. It's easier to find places, more organized.
2. Answers will vary.
3. Possible answers: bring more jobs and tax money; pollution, more traffic
4. Answers will vary.
5. Answers will vary.
6. Answers will vary.
7. Answers will vary.

Page 41:
1. Florida
2. Alaska
3. Gulf of Mexico
4. Arkansas
5. Utah
6. Delaware
7. New Mexico
8. Nebraska
9. Washington
10. Lake Michigan
11. Maine
12. Kentucky

Page 42:
1. 0 to 500 feet
2. Rio Grande
3. 5,000 to 10,000 feet
4. peninsula
5. northern; western
6. 20°N, 90°W
7. More than 10,000 feet
8. Guadalajara

Page 43:
1. Check to see that students complete the key correctly.
2. Independence
3. west, then southwest
4. Gila River Trail, Old Spanish Trail
5. Platte
6. became higher
7. Great Salt Lake
8. Portland: Oregon Trail; San Diego: Gila River Trail; Sacramento: California Trail

Page 44: